CW00405330

An Introduction to
the Life and Works of
GEORGE FOX

An Introduction to
the Life and Works of
GEORGE FOX

Christian Barclay

BISHOPSGATE PRESS

© 1989 Christian Barclay

British Library Cataloguing in Publication Data
Barclay, Christian
George, Fox.
1. Society of Friends. Fox, George, 1624-1691
I. Title
289.6'0924

ISBN 1-85219-080-9

All rights reserved. No part of this publication may be reproduced, stored in a retrieval system, or transmitted, in any form or by any means, electrical, mechanical, photocopying, recording or otherwise, without the prior permission of the copyright owner.

All enquiries and requests relevant to this title should be sent to the publisher, Bishopsgate Press Ltd., 37, Union Street, London SE1 1SE

Printed by Whitstable Printers Ltd., Millstrood Road, Whitstable, Kent

Contents

Acknowlegements.

The 'Compiler' wishes to thank Cecil Sharman for permission to quote from his book 'No More But My Love'. George Target for continuing encouragement and Margaret Richter for her skilful typing and advice.

George Fox 1624-1691

George Fox was the founder of the Religious Society of Friends, generally known as the Quakers. His life spanned the greater part of the 17th century, a period as tumultuous as our own in events and ideas. Politically the ruling power was changing from King to People, that is to say the people of the propertied classes, but in the underlying world of ideas the revolution affected the whole of society. In the previous century Henry VIII had made use of the Reformation for his political ends, but he was thereafter unable to stem the incoming tide of ideas. Once remove the authority of the Roman church, make the Bible available for all to read, and the individual reader will make his own interpretation of the Christian religion. That interpretation laid increasing emphasis on aspects of the teaching of Christ that had become buried under stultifying doctrine.

In previous centuries the "common man" had made attempts, basing his claim on Christ's teaching, to assert his rights and his dignity. These attempts were stifled or forced underground. Not until the 17th century did events contrive to give them real political weight.

Men were enrolled into the New Model Army to fight for freedom, but the interpretation of that freedom depended on the class of society from which the soldiers were drawn. Ideas spread among this mobile force. Levellers, Diggers, Fifth Monarchy Men were all among those who wanted to see the political revolution go further than the propertied leaders intended, and most based their ideas upon aspects of the Gospel teaching which those in power would have preferred to overlook. All this has to be borne in mind in order to understand why Fox met with such hostility from his contemporaries. He claimed Christ's authority for all his teaching, but his deductions scared those who saw the political implications which might be involved.

In 1643, the year that Cromwell was recruiting his New Model Army, George Fox, then a young man of 19, set out on a more lonely adventure. He had always been a thoughtful lad, brought up in a good honest home, and he cared desperately for truth in all things. He tells that his neighbours used to say of him, "If George says 'Verily', there is no altering him." It was this passion for the truth in all things that drove him out in his search for reality in religion. Where could he find those who really practised what they preached? So many "professors" (of religion) were coldhearted and insincere. The crisis came for him when some cousins, said to be "professors", tried to involve him in a drinking bout. He was utterly shocked. After a night of torment and prayer he felt that the Lord was telling him to "forsake all and be a stranger to all", and so he left home and started wandering over the Midlands trying to find someone who would understand his distress.

His searching and wanderings, in great distress of mind, lasted four years. No one seemed to understand him. Some, thinking to divert him, suggested he took tobacco, and his relations advised him to marry. No one accepted the reality of his inner conflict. Gradually it came to him with growing conviction that God had given him the answer within himself.

> And when my hope in them and all men were
> gone, so that I had nothing outwardly to help
> me, nor could tell what to do, oh then I heard a
> voice which said, "There is one even Christ
> Jesus that can speak to thy condition", and
> when I heard it my heart did leap for joy.

After that, in spite of setbacks, he grew increasingly strong in his conviction that God had sent him to share with all men his discovery of the Light of Christ within and to persuade them to turn to that light for fullness of life.

He journeyed further afield and by 1652 he reached the Dales of Yorkshire. There one day he was moved to climb Pendle Hill, from which he saw his vision of a "great people to be gathered". In these northern parts he came across "the Seekers", little groups of people who like him were dissatisfied with the religious teaching and practise of the day and were waiting for a new revelation. These groups flocked to hear him. Then, at Swarthmore Hall, the home of Judge Fell near Ulverstone, he met the Judge's wife Margaret and her large family. He was welcomed there and Margaret persuaded her husband to invite him to preach in the house, and later to offer him a refuge and basis for his work. For the next ten years, it became a power house and resting place for the growing Society, and it was from this district that George Fox organised the body of young men, who later became known as the "Valiant Sixty", who helped to spread the teaching all over the country.

The decade of the Commonwealth saw Quakerism

established all over the British Isles and spread into Europe and the American colonies. But in 1656 a tragic event occured which shook the foundations of the growing Society. James Naylor, one of the Valiant Sixty, and a brilliant preacher, allowed two hysterical women to stage his entry into Bristol riding on an ass. This was meant as a sign of the coming of Christ, but the authorities not unnaturally considered it dangerous blasphemy and took the opportunity to make an example of the growing sect. They brought Naylor to London, where he was tried before Parliament and punished with horrible severity. He died soon afterward humbled and deeply penitent for the harm he had done. Through this incident Fox was encouraged to face the fact that fallible individuals could mistake God's guidance and "run out into imaginings". Thereafter, he stressed increasingly the importance of the gathered Meeting as a curb on the more exuberant and less stable of his followers. Moreover, fierce persecution and imprisonment were disrupting the lives of those who were true to his teaching, and a close fellowship of Friends was needed for mutual caring and support. Fox had always maintained that the "Church" was not the building — he called that the "steeple house". The true Church was the body of the followers of Christ, and thereafter he used increasingly his remarkable organising ability to form a flexible system of church government, which has indeed endured to this day.

There is no doubt that Fox's appearance and manner invited hostility. His leather breeches and shaggy hair provoked comments and jibes, as indeed did the way in which Quakers in their Meeting would sit so long in silence waiting on God. When Fox did speak, his merciless fulminations against hypocrisy, "steeple houses", and "hireling priests" infuriated the crowds, at the same time as many were petrified by his piercing eyes. Yet, as he became known for his courage and integrity, many of his antagonists were forced to admit their admiration for him: "He is as stiff as a tree and pure as a bell, for we could never stir him."

When one reads accounts of Friends being brought before courts of law it is clear that there were three main sources of controversy. Their refusal to remove their hats before authority, based as it was on the conviction that such deference should be given to God alone, nevertheless struck magistrates as provocative rudeness. Then there were Fox's invectives against the established church and the payment of priests for preaching what should be a "free gospel". This, of course, led to direct conflict in the refusal to pay tithes. The non-payment of tithes brought Quakers into line with many other of the more politically-based sects of the day, and so more deeply under suspicion.

What gave the authorities their sure chance to arrest was the refusal to take an oath. Fox asserted that Christ had forbidden his followers to swear; their "yea" was to be "yea" and their "nay", "nay", and this was according to Bible teaching. (He once suggested they should imprison the Bible instead of him!) But for mid-17th century justices and magistrates, always nervously on the lookout for conspiracies, any man would be suspect who, being capable of bringing great crowds together under his influence, would then refuse to swear allegiance to the government or king. The Clarendon Code, after the abortive rising of the Fifth Monarchy men in 1661, gave legal justification for imprisonments, fines and praemunire, and fierce persecution of Quakers went on until the Act of Toleration was passed in 1689, two years before Fox died.

He was himself, in his later years, greatly debilitated and often severely ill as a result of the terrible experiences he had had in prison, and during his adventurous journeyings in America, where he savoured the full rigors of early colonial life.

In 1669 he married Judge Fell's widow Margaret, who with her daughters and family at Swarthmore had always supported him and provided him with a loving home when his work allowed him to rest. Margaret Fell's life is a story in itself and exemplifies magnificently the part that Fox realised women could play in the Society of Friends.

During the latter part of his life Fox wrote a great deal. He dictated his *Journal*, which is in fact a detailed autobiography and not only provides a vivid account of early Quaker history, but gives fascinating insight into the lives of ordinary men and women during the mid-17th century. It was prepared for publication by Thomas Ellwood, and others of his followers, shortly after his death. He also himself wrote many "epistles", letters of encouragement to Friends and Meetings all over the known world. These letters show the deeply concerned and loving side of his nature. His readers would know, when he encouraged them in resistance to authority, that he never advocated any line of action which he had not previously taken, with all its consequences, on himself. He never ceased to assert that the love of God abounded and was worth it all. As he lay dying and friends came to enquire after him, he said "Never heed, the Lord's power is over all weakness and death, the seed reigns, blessed be the Lord."

His great friend and follower, William Penn, added at the last, "Many souls have done virtuously in their day, but thou, dear George, thou excellest them all."

Seeking And Finding

I was still under great temptations sometimes, and my inward sufferings were heavy; but I could find none to open my condition to but the Lord alone, unto whom I cried night and day. I went back into Nottinghamshire, and there the Lord shewed me that the nature of those things which were hurtful without, were within, in the hearts and minds of wicked men. I cried to the Lord, saying, "Why should I be thus, seeing I was never addicted to commit those evils?" and the Lord answered that it was needful I should have a sense of all conditions, how else should I speak to all conditions, and in this I saw the infinite love of God. I saw also that there was an ocean of darkness and death, but an infinite ocean of light and love which flowed over the ocean of darkness. In that also I saw the infinite love of God; and I had great openings.

Journal p 11 (1647)

Though my exercises and troubles were very great, yet were they not so continual but that I had some intermissions, and was sometimes brought into such a heavenly joy, that I thought I had been in Abraham's bosom. As I cannot declare the misery I was in, it was so great and heavy upon me, so neither can I set forth the mercies of God unto me in all my misery. Oh, the everlasting love of God to my soul when I was in great distress! When my troubles and torments were great, then was His love exceeding great.

Journal p 8 (1647)

Now I was come up in spirit through the flaming sword, into the paradise of God. All things were new; and all the creation gave another smell unto me than before, beyond what words can utter. I knew nothing but pureness, and innocency, and righteousness, being renewed up into the image of God by Christ Jesus, to the state of Adam, which he was in before the fall. . . . Great things did the Lord lead me into, and wonderful depths were opened unto me beyond what can by words be declared; but as people come into subjection to the Spirit of God and grow up in the image and power of the Almighty, they may receive the word of wisdom, that opens all things, and come to know the hidden unity in the Eternal Being.

Journal p 17 (1649)

. . .And one morning, as I was sitting by the fire, a great cloud came over me, and a temptation beset me; but I sate still. And it was said, "All things come by nature"; and the elements and stars came over me, so that I was in a manner quite clouded with it. But in as much as I sate still and silent the people of the house perceived nothing. And as I sate still under it and let it alone, a living hope arose in me, and a true voice, which said, "There is a living God who made all things." And immediately the cloud and temptation vanished away, and life rose over it all; my heart was glad, and I praised the living God. After some time, I met with some people who had such a notion that there was no God, but that all things came by nature. I had great dispute with them and overturned them and made some of them confess that there is a living God. Then I saw that it was good that I had gone through that exercise.

Journal p 15 (1648)

As we travelled we came near a very great hill, called Pendle Hill, and I was moved of the Lord to go up to the top of it; which I did with great difficulty, it was so very steep and high. When I was come to the top, I saw the sea bordering upon Lancashire, and there, on the top, I was moved to sound the day of the Lord, and the Lord let me see in what places He had a great people to be gathered.

Journal p 60 (1652)

...I was sent to turn people from darkness to the light that they might receive Christ Jesus; for, to as many as should receive Him in His light, I saw that he would give power to become the sons of God; which I had obtained by receiving Christ. And I was to direct people to the Spirit that gave forth the Scriptures, by which they might be led into all Truth, and so up to Christ and God, as they had been who gave them forth. And I was to turn them to the grace of God, and the truth in the heart, which came by Jesus;... I was to bring people off from all their own ways to Christ, the new and living way... to know the spirit of Truth in the inward parts, and to be led thereby, that in it they might worship the Father of Spirit... making melody in their hearts to the Lord who hath sent his beloved son to be the Saviour, and caused his heavenly sun to shine upon all the world, and through them all, and his heavenly rain to fall upon the just and the unjust (as his outward rain doth fall, and his outward sun doth shine on all), which is God's unspeakable love to the world.

Journal (1648) - quoted in
Christian Faith and Practice Sect.10

His Sufferings

...While I was at Mansfield Woodhouse, I was moved to go to the steeple-house there on a First-day... and declare the truth to the priests and people; but the people fell upon me in great rage, struck me down, and almost stifled and smothered me; and I was cruelly beaten and bruised by them with their hands, Bibles and sticks. Then they haled me out, though I was hardly able to stand, and put me into the stocks, where I sate some hours and they brought dog-whips and horse-whips, threatening to whip me, and as I sate in the stocks they threw stones at me. After some time they had me before the Magistrate ... where were many great persons; who, seeing how evilly I had been used, after much threatening set me at liberty. But the rude people stoned me out of town, and threatened me with pistols, for preaching the word of life to them. I was scarce able to move or stand, by reason of the ill usage I had received ... but the Lord's power went through me and healed me. That day some people were convinced of the Lord's truth, and turned to His teaching, at which I rejoiced.

Journal pp 26-27 (1649)

Prison - At Scarborough Castle,
(one of many such imprisonments)

...I desired the Governor to go into my room, and see what a place I had. I had got a little fire made in it and it was so filled with smoke that when he was in it he could hardly find his way out again; and he being a Papist I told him it was his Purgatory they had put me into. I was forced to lay out a matter of 50 shillings to stop out the rain and keep the room from smoking so much. When I had been at that charge, and made the room somewhat tolerable, they removed me into a worse room, where I had neither chimney nor fire-hearth. This being to the sea-side and lying much open, the wind drove in the rain forcibly, so that the water came over my bed, and ran about the room, and I was fain to skim it up with a platter. And when my clothes were wet, I had no fire to dry them; so that my body was numbed with cold, and my fingers swelled, that one was grown as big as two. Though I was at some charge on this room also, I could not keep out the wind and rain.

Journal pp 237-8 (1665)

Fox's Impact On Others

Now the time of my commitment to the House of Correction being nearly out, and there being many new soldiers raised, the commissioners would have made me captain over them, and the soldiers cried they would have none but me. So the keeper of the House of Correction was commanded to bring me before the commissioners and soldiers in the market place; and there they offered me that preferment (as they called it) asking me if I would not take up arms for the Commonwealth against Charles Stuart? I told them I knew from whence all wars arose, even from the lust, according to James' doctrine; and that I lived in the virtue of that life and power that took away the occasion of all wars. But they courted me to accept their offer, and thought I did but compliment with them. But I told them I was come into the covenant of peace which was before wars and strifes were.

Journal pp 35-6 (1650)

... At another place I heard some of the magistrates say among themselves that if they had money enough they would hire me to be their minister. This was where they did not well understand us and our principles; but when I heard of it I said "It is time for me to be gone; for if their eye is so much to me, or any of us, they will not come to their own teacher." For this thing (of hiring ministers) had spoiled many by hindering them from improving their own talents; whereas our labour is to bring all men to their own Teacher in themselves.

Journal p 290 (1672)

While I was in prison in Launceston, a Friend went to O.C.* and offered his body to lie in Doomsdale in my stead, if he would take him, and let me have liberty. Which thing so struck him, that he said to his great men and Council "Which of you would do so much for me if I were in the same condition?" And though he did not accept of the Friend's offer, but said he could not do it, for that it was contrary to law, yet the truth thereby came mightily over him.

Journal p 135 (1656)

* Oliver Cromwell

Meetings with Oliver Cromwell and Others

But the next morning I was moved of the Lord to write a paper "To the Protector by the name of Oliver Cromwell," wherein I did in the presence of the Lord God declare that I did deny the wearing or drawing of a carnal sword, or any other outward weapon against him or any man: and that I was sent of God to stand a witness against all violence, and against the works of darkness; and to turn people from darkness to light;

and to bring them from the occasion of war and fighting to the peaceable gospel, and from being evil-doers which the magistrates' swords should be a terror to . . . .

Then after some time Captain Drury brought me before the Protector himself at Whitehall. . . . When I came in I was moved to say, "Peace be in this house"; and I bid him to keep in the fear of God, that he might receive wisdom from Him, that by it he might be directed, and order all things under his hand to God's glory. I spake much to him of Truth, and much discourse I had with him about religion; wherein he carried himself very moderately . . . . I told him that all Christendom (so called) possessed the Scriptures, but wanted the power and Spirit that they had who gave forth the Scriptures, and that was the reason they were not in fellowship with the Son, or with the Father, or with the Scriptures, or with one another.

Many more words I had with him, but people coming in, I drew a little back; and as I was turning he caught my by the hand and with tears in his eyes, said, "Come again to my house, for if thou and I were but an hour of a day together, we should be nearer one to the other"; adding that he wished me no more ill than he did his own soul. I told him if he did he wronged his own soul; and I bid him hearken to God's voice, that he might stand in His counsel and obey it; and if he did so, that would keep him from hardness of heart; but if he did not hear God's voice, his heart would be hardened. He said it was true.

Journal p 105 (1654)

During the time I was in London, many services lay upon me: for it was time of much suffering. I was moved to write to Oliver Cromwell, and lay before him the sufferings of Friends, both in this nation and in Ireland. There was also talk about this time of making Cromwell king; whereupon I was moved to go to him. I met him in the Park and told him that they that would put him on a crown would take away his life . . . and I bid him mind the crown that was immortal. He thanked me, and bid me go to his house. Afterwards I was moved to write to him more fully concerning that matter. . . .

[Another day], taking boat, I went to Kingston, and thence to Hampton Court, to speak with the Protector about the sufferings of Friends.

I met him riding into Hampton Court Park, and before I came to him, as he rode at the head of his life-guard, I saw and felt a waft of death go forth against him; and when I came to him he looked like a dead man. After I had laid the sufferings of Friends before him, and had warned him, according as I was moved to speak to him, he bid me come to his house. So . . . the next day I went to Hampton Court, to speak further with him. But when I came he was very sick, and [they] told me the Doctors were not willing I should speak with him. So I passed away, and never saw him more.

Journal pp 171-173 (1658)

... When we were come to the mayor's house, and were brought into the room where he was, I was brought up to the table where he sate; and then the officers took off my hat; and the mayor said mildly to me, "Mr Fox, you are an eminent man among those of your profession; pray will you be instrumental to dissuade them from meeting in such great numbers? for, seeing Christ hath promised that where two or three are met in His name, He will be in the midst of them, and the King and Parliament are graciously pleased to allow of four to meet together to worship God, why will not you be content to partake both of Christ's promise to two or three, and the King's indulgence to four?" I wished him to consider whether this Act would not have taken hold of Christ, with his twelve apostles and seventy disciples, if it had been in their time, who used to meet often together, and that with great numbers. However, I told him this Act did not concern us; for it was made against seditious meetings, of such as met under colour and pretence of religion to contrive insurrections, as (the Act says) late experience has shewn; but we had been sufficiently tried and proved, and always found peaceable, and therefore he should do well to put a difference between the innocent and the guilty.... Therefore, we being innocent, and not the people this Act concerns, we keep our meetings as we used to do: and, I said, I believed that he knew in his conscience we were innocent. After some more discourse he took our names and the places where we lodged, and at length set us at liberty.

Journal p 266 (1670)

Sickness And Healings

About this time the Lady Claypole [Elizabeth Cromwell, second daughter of the Protector] was very sick and troubled in mind, and nothing could comfort her; which when I heard of, I was moved to write to her. ... When the paper was read to her, she said it settled and staid her mind for the present. Afterwards many Friends got copies of it both in England and Ireland, and read it to distracted people, and it was made useful for the settling of the minds of several.

Journal pp 171-172 (1658)

Coming to Mansfield Woodhouse, there was a distracted woman under a doctor's hand, with her hair loose all about her ears. He was about to bleed her, she being first bound, and many people being about her, holding her by violence; but he could get no blood from her. I desired them unbind her, and let her alone, for they could not touch the spirit in her, by which she was tormented. So they unbound her; and I was moved to speak to her, and in the name of the Lord to bid her be quiet and still; and she was so. The Lord's power settled her mind and she mended; and afterwards she received the truth, and continued in it to her death. The Lord's name was honoured; to whom the glory of all his works belongs.

Journal pp 26-27 (1649)

[After his death in prison] ... Friends told me that Edward Burroughs said if he had been but an hour with me he should have been well.

Journal p 206 (1662)

And as I came out of Cumberland, one time, I came to Hawkeshead, and lighted at a Friend's house. And there was young Margaret Fell with me and William Caton. And it being a very cold season, we lighted, and the lass made us a fire, her master and dame being gone to market. And there was a boy lying in the cradle which they rocked, about eleven years old. And he was grown almost double. And I cast my eye upon the boy; and seeing he was dirty, I bid the lass wash his face and his hands, and get him up and bring him unto me. So she brought him to me, and I bid her take him and wash him again, for she had not washed him clean. Then was I moved of the Lord God to lay my hands upon him and speak to him, and so bid the lass take him again and put on his clothes. And after we passed away.

And sometimes after I called at the house, and I met his mother but did not light. "Oh! stay," says she "and have a meeting at our house, for all the country is convinced by the great miracle that was done by thee upon my son. For we had carried him to Wells and the Bath, and all doctors had given him over, for his grandfather and father feared he would have died and their name have gone out, having but that son; but presently, after you were gone," says she, "we came home and found our son playing in the streets. Therefore," said she, "all the country would come to hear," if I would come back again and have a meeting there. And this was about three years after she told me of it, and he was grown to be a straight, full youth then. So the Lord have the praise.

Journal pp 92-93 (1653)

The Church

... He asked me what a church was? I told him the Church was the pillar and ground of Truth, made up of living stones, living members, a spiritual household, which Christ was the head of: but He was not the head of a mixed multitude, or of an old house made up of lime, stones, and wood. This set them all on fire.

Journal pp 14-15 (1648)

... I went into the steeple-house and sate me down till the priest had done. The words which he took for his text were these, "Ho, every one that thirsteth, come ye to the waters; and he that hath no money, come ye, buy and eat, yea come, buy wine and milk without money and without price." Then I was moved of the Lord to say unto him, "Come down, thou deceiver; dost thou bid people come freely, and take of the water of life freely, and yet thou takes three hundred pounds a-year of them, for preaching the Scriptures to them! Mayst thou not blush for shame! Did the prophet Isaiah and Christ do so, who spake the words, and gave them forth freely? Did not Christ say to His ministers, whom He sent to preach, 'Freely ye have received, freely give'?" The priest, like a man amazed, packed away.

Journal p 43 (1651)

We need no Mass for to teach us, and we need not your Common Prayer, for the Spirit that gave forth the Scriptures teacheth us how to pray, sing, fast and to give thanks; and how to honour and glorify God, and how to walk before him and men; and how to use all creatures upon earth. . . .

. . . And men stand in doubts and questions, and have no assurance in their religion, but that of God stands in them all bound. Our faith, our church, our unity is the Spirit, and our Word at which we tremble was in the beginning before your Church-made faiths, and our unity, church and fellowship will stand when they are all ended.

Letter 75 Ep. 171 (1659)

The Priests and professors of all sorts were much against Friends' silent Meetings; and sometimes the priests and professors would come to our meetings and when they saw one hundred or two hundred people all silent, waiting upon the Lord, they would break out into wonder and despising, and some of them would say, "Look how these people sit mumbing and dumbing! what edification is here where there are no words? Come," would they say, "let us be gone. Why should we stay here to see a people sit in this manner?" And they said they never saw the like in their life.

Then, it may be, some Friends have been moved to speak to them, and say, "Didst thou never see the like in thy life? Look in thy own parish and let the priest see there, how your people 'sit mumbing and dumbing' and sleeping under your priests all their life-time, who keep people always under their teaching that they may be always paying."

Journal p 211 (1663)

Concerning Tithes

So all ye that are summoned with writs to answer because ye cannot pay tithes, keep to the Light in you. And so, according to the Light of Christ in them all, speak, that to it their minds may be guided; and declare the truth to them, which is agreeable to that of God in every one's conscience. And declare it to the highest judicature in the nation that ye suffer for the testimony of Jesus, and that ye witness to the ministry of Life. . . . And so, if the spoilers take your goods, let them go, and let them take the coat also.

. . . To the Light of Christ Jesus in all your consciences I speak, that ye may see what ye act, and that such as are sued for tithes may look to the unchangable priest, Christ Jesus.

Letter 37 Ep. 73 (1654)

The Bible

As we travelled through the country, preaching repentance to the people, the Lord said unto me, if that I did but set up one in the same spirit that the prophets and apostles were in that gave forth the Scriptures, he or she should shake all the country in their profession ten miles about them. And if they did own God and Christ and His prophets and apostles they must own him or her. For people had the Scriptures, but were not in that same light, and power, and spirit which they were in that gave forth the Scriptures; and so they neither knew God, nor Christ, nor the Scriptures aright; nor had they unity one with another, being out of the power and spirit of God.

Journal p 59 (1652)

. . . the Holy Scriptures were given forth by the Spirit of God, and all people must first come to the Spirit of God in themselves, by which they might know God and Christ, of whom the prophets and apostles learnt; and by the same spirit know the Holy Scriptures; for as the Spirit of God was in them that gave forth the Scriptures, so the same Spirit of God must be in all them that come to understand the Scriptures; by which Spirit they might have fellowship with the Son, and with the Father, and with the Scriptures, and with one another; and without this Spirit they can know neither God nor Christ, nor the Scriptures, nor have right fellowship one with another.

Journal p 78 (1652)

Friend's Response To Persecution

It was a time of great sufferings; for besides the imprisonments (through which many died in prisons) our meetings were greatly disturbed. They have thrown rotten eggs and wild-fire into our meetings, and have brought in drums beating, and kettles to make noises with, that the truth might not be heard; and among these the priests were as rude as any.

Journal p 174 (1658)

... So we rode to Leicester, being five in number; some carried their Bibles open in their hands, declaring the truth to the people as we rode, in the fields and through the towns, and telling them we were prisoners of the Lord Jesus Christ, going to suffer bonds for His name and truth's sake. One woman Friend carried her wheel on her lap to spin on in prison; and the people were mightily affected.

Journal p 203 (1662)

Now it was a time of great suffering; and many Friends being in prisons, many other Friends were moved to go to the Parliament, to offer up themselves to lie in the same dungeons where their friends lay, that they that were in prison might go out, and not perish in the stinking jails. This we did in love to God and our brethren, that they might not die in prison; and love to those that cast them in, that they might not bring innocent blood upon their own heads; which we knew would cry to the Lord, and bring His wrath, vengeance, and plagues upon them. But little favour could we find from those professing Parliaments; instead thereof they would rage, and sometimes threaten those Friends that thus attended them that they would whip them, and send them home.

Journal p 172 (1658)

There seemed at that time an inclination and intention in the Government to grant Friends liberty, because they were sensible that we had suffered as well as they under the former powers. . . . It was said there was an instrument drawn up for confirming our liberty, and that it only wanted signing; when, suddenly, the wicked attempt of the Fifth-monarchy people broke out, and put the City and nation in an uproar. . . . Great mischief was done in the City this week; and when the next First-day came, as Friends went to their meetings many were taken prisoner.

Journal p 193 (1661)

. . . Friends told us how they had broken up their Meetings by warrants from the justices, and how by their warrants they were required to carry Friends before the justices; and Friends bid them carry them then. The officers said nay; they must go: but Friends said nay; that was not according to their warrants, which required them to carry them. Then they were fain to hire carts, and waggons, and horses and to lift Friends up into their waggons and carts, to carry them before a justice. When they came to a justice's house, sometimes he happened to be from home, and if he were a moderate man he would, it may be, get out of the way, and then they were obliged to carry them before another, so that they were almost three weeks carting and carrying Friends up and down from place to place. And when afterwards the officers came to lay their charges for this upon the town, the town's-people would not pay it, but made them bear it themselves; which brake the neck of their persecution there for that time.

Journal p 213 (1663)

Several other Friends were committed to prison, some for meeting to worship God, and some for not swearing; so that the prison was very full. Many of them being poor men that had nothing to maintain their families by but their labour which now they were taken off from, several of their wives went to the justices who had committed their husbands, and told them if they kept their husbands in jail for nothing but the truth of Christ, and good conscience sake, they would bring their children to the justices for them to maintain them. A mighty power of the Lord rose in Friends, and gave them great boldness, so that they spake much to the justices. Friends also that were prisoners wrote to the justices, laying the weight of their sufferings upon them, and shewing them both their injustice and want of compassion towards their poor neighbours, whom they knew to be honest, conscientious, peaceable people, that in tenderness of conscience could not take any oath; yet they sent them to prison for refusing to take the oath of Allegiance. Several who were imprisoned on that account were known to be men that had served the King in his wars, and had hazarded their lives in the field in his cause, . . . and had always stood faithful to him from first to last, and had never received any pay for their service. To be thus requited for all their faithful services and sufferings, and that by them that pretended to be the King's friends, was hard, unkind, and ungrateful dealing. At length the justices being continually attended with complaints of grievances, released some of the Friends, but kept divers of them still in prison.

Journal pp 223-224 (1663)

Organisation Of The Society Of Friends

After some time we came to John Crook's house, where a general Yearly Meeting for the whole nation was appointed to be held. This meeting lasted three days, and many Friends from most parts of the nation came to it; so that the inns and towns around were filled, for many thousands of people were at it. And although there was some disturbance by rude people that had run out from the Truth, yet the Lord's power came over all, and a glorious meeting it was. The everlasting gospel was preached, and many received it, which brought life and immortality to light in them, and shined over all.

Journal p 168 (1658)

From Balby I passed to Skipton, where there was a General Meeting of men Friends out of many counties, concerning the affairs of the Church. To this Meeting came some Friends out of most parts of the nation; for it was about business relating to the Church both in this nation and beyond the seas.

Several years before, when I was in the North, I was moved to recommend the setting up of this Meeting for that service; for many Friends suffered in divers parts of the nation, their goods were taken from them contrary to the law, and they understood not how to help themselves or where to seek redress. But after this Meeting was set up, several Friends who had been magistrates, and others that understood something of the law, came thither, and were able to inform Friends, and to assist them in gathering up the sufferings, that they might be laid before the justices, judges or Parliament. This Meeting had stood several years, and divers justices and captains had come to break it up; but when they understood the business Friends met about, and saw their books and accounts of collections for the relief of the poor, how we took care one county to help another, and to help our Friends beyond the seas, and provide for our poor that none of them should be chargeable to their parishes, etc, the justices and officers confessed we did their work, and passed away peaceably and lovingly, commending Friends' practice.

Journal p 183-184 (1660)

Then I was moved of the Lord God to set up and establish five monthly meetings of men and women in the City of London (besides the women's meetings and the quarterly meeting), to take care of God's glory, and to admonish and exhort such as walked disorderly or carelessly, and not according to Truth. For whereas Friends had had only quarterly meetings, now Truth was spread and Friends were grown more numerous, I was moved to recommend the setting up of monthly meetings throughout the nation. And the Lord opened to me and let me see what I must do, and how I must order the men's and women's monthly and quarterly meetings and establish them in this and in other nations; and that I should write to those where I came not, to do the same.

Journal p 249 (1667)

Women

At Slaughterford, in Wiltshire, we had a very good meeting, though we met there with much opposition from some who had set themselves against women's meetings; which I was moved of the Lord to recommend to Friends, for the benefit and advantage of the Church of Christ. . . . That so all the family of God, women as well as men, might know, possess, perform and discharge their offices and services in the house of God, whereby the poor might be better taken care of and looked after, and the younger sort instructed, informed and taught in the way of God; the loose and disorderly reproved and admonished in the fear of the Lord; the clearness of persons pronouncing marriage more strictly and closely enquired into in the wisdom of God; and all the members of the spiritual body, the Church, might watch over and be helpful to each other in love.

Journal p 314 (1673)

Some there have been that would not have the women to speak without the men; and some of them say the women must not speak in the Church. And if they must not speak, what should they meet with them for? What a spirit is this, that will neither suffer the women to speak amongst the men, nor to meet amongst themselves to speak? For the power and spirit of God gives liberty to all; for women are heirs of life as well as the men, and heirs of Grace, and of the Light of Christ Jesus, as well as the men, and so stewards of the manifold grace of God.

... the women in their assemblies may inform one another of the poor widows and fatherless, and in the wisdom of God may find the best way for the setting forth of their children, and to see that their children are preserved in the Truth, and instruct them in the fear of the Lord. And if there were no Scripture for our Men and Women's Meetings, Christ is sufficient, who restores men and women up to the image of God.

Letter 109 Ep. 320 (1676)

After this I met with a sort of people that held women had no souls, adding, in a light manner, no more than a goose. But I reproved them, and told them that was not right; for Mary said "My soul doth magnify the Lord, and my spirit hath rejoiced in God my saviour."

Journal p 7 (1647)

Concerning the Women's Meetings: encourage all the women of families, that are convinced and mind virtue, and love Truth and walk in it, they may come up into God's service, that they may be serviceable in their generation and come into the practice of the pure religion, that every one may come to know their duty in it, and their service in the power and wisdom of God. For people must not always be talking and hearing, but they must come into obedience to the great God of heaven and earth.

And so, that none may stand idle out of the vineyard, and out of the service, and out of their duty, (for such will talk and tattle and judge with evil thoughts what they in the vineyard say and do), the power of the Lord God calls all into their duty and service. For all that are out of this, though they may have the knowledge of it, yet are not serviceable in the creation, nor in their generation. . . .

And make all the sober women, both of town and country, acquainted with this thing. And read this in your Monthly Meetings.

So, no more but my love.

G.F. 1666
Letter 90 Ep. 248

Marriage

... He said ... "You marry, but I know not how." I replied, "It may be so; but why dost thou not come and see?" ... I asked him where he read from Genesis to the Revelations that ever any priest did marry any. And I wished him to shew me some instance there of, if he would have us come to them to be married; "for," said I, "thou has excommunicated one of my friends, two years after he was dead, about his marriage. And why dost thou not excommunicate Isaac, and Jacob, and Boaz, and Ruth? Why dost thou not use thy power against these? for we do not read that they were ever married by the priests; but they took one another in the assemblies of the righteous, in the presence of God and His people; and so do we. So that we have all the holy men and women, that the Scripture speaks of in this practise, on our side."

Journal p 243 (1666)

... I was moved to open to the people the state of our marriages, declaring how the people of God took one another in the assemblies of the Elders, and that it was God who joined man and woman together before the fall. ... but never any priest did marry any, that we read of in the Scriptures from Genesis to the Revelations. Then I shewed them the duty of man and wife, how they should serve God, being heirs of life and grace together.

Journal p 246 (1666)

Education And Upbringing Of Children

His own experience

When I was elven years of age I knew pureness and righteousness; for while a child I was taught to walk to be kept pure. The Lord taught me to be Faithful in all things, and to act faithfully two ways, viz., inwardly to God, and outwardly to man; and to keep to Yea and Nay in all things. For the Lord shewed me, that though the people of the world have mouths full of deceit, and changeable words, yet I was to keep to Yea and Nay in all things; and that my words should be few and savoury, seasoned with grace; and that I might not eat and drink to make myself wanton, but for health, using the creatures in their service, as servants in their places, to the glory of Him that created them, they being in their covenant, and I being brought up into the covenant, as sanctified by the Word which was in the beginning, by which all things are upheld; wherein is unity with the creations.

Journal pp 1-2 (1635)

Schools founded

... Then, returning towards London by Waltham, I advised the setting up of a school there for teaching children; and also a women's school at Shacklewell, for instructing young lassies and maidens in whatsoever things were civil and useful in the creation.

Journal p 252 (1668)

It's desired, that all Friends, that have children, families and servants, may train them up in the pure and unspotted religion, and in the nurture and fear of God, and that frequently they may read the holy Scriptures, which is much better than to be gadding abroad. And exhort and admonish them that every family apart may serve and worship the Lord, as well as in public. And that when they go to Meetings they may take their families and servants with them, that they may not go wandering up and down in the fields, or to ale-houses, as many have done, to the dishonour of God, and to dishonour of their masters' and mistresses' families, and to their own ruin and destruction. And therefore, for Christ's sake, and his pure religion, let there be care taken to prevent all these things. For such a one as cannot rule well his own house, having his children in subjection with all due gravity, how can he take care of the church of God?

Letter 128 Ep. 389 (1683)

All Friends and people,

No man after he hath beaten his child, hateth him ever afterwards, but loveth him, if he repent and amends; so doth the eternal Father. And if the child be fallen down into the dirt, he doth not go and tumble him more into the dirt, or into the ditch, and there let him lie in the dirt and ditch, but takes him out and washes him; and so doth the heavenly Father, which leads his children by his hand, and dandles them upon his knee. And so, all that be called fathers in the Truth, or mothers, their tenderness should be the same to all little children in the Truth, that can hardly go without leading, and sometimes may fall into the dirt and ditch, and slip aside, and then be troubled and cry. To such there should be tenderness shown, to wash them, and help them. And love to such should be manifest; for there is a difference between a stubborn, rebellious and wilful child, and one that is penitent; for those must have great chastisements and stripes, that knows the will of their Father and does it not.

Letter 94 Ep. 262 (1668)

Wider Social Concerns

In this time of my imprisonment I was exceedingly exercised about the proceeding of the judges and magistrates in their Courts of judicature. I was moved to write to the judges concerning their putting men to death for cattle, and money, and small matters; and to shew them how contrary it was to the law of God in old time.

... Moreover I laid before the judges what a sore thing it was that prisoners should lie so long in jail, shewing how they learned badness one of another in talking of their bad deeds; and therefore speedy justice should be done.

Journal pp 37-38 (1651)

At a certain time, when I was at Mansfield, there was a sitting of the justices about hiring of servants; and it was upon me from the Lord to go and speak to the justices, that they should not oppress the servants in their wages ... and I exhorted the servants to do their duties, and serve honestly etc.

... I was moved to go to several Courts and steeple-houses ... to warn them to leave off oppression and oaths, and to turn from deceit and to turn to the Lord, and to do justly.

Journal p 16 (1648)

Cornish Wreckers

While I was in Cornwall there were great shipwrecks about the Land's End. Now it was the custom of that country, that at such a time both rich and poor went out to get as much of the wreck as they could, not caring to save the people's lives; and in some places they call shipwrecks "God's grace." These things troubled me; it grieved my spirit to hear of such unchristian actions. Wherefore I was moved to write a paper, and send it to all the parishes, priests and magistrates, to reprove them for such greedy actions, and to warn and exhort them that, if they could assist to save people's lives and preserve their ships and goods, they should use their diligence therein; and consider, if it had been their own condition they would judge it hard if they should be upon a wreck and people should strive to get what they could from them, and not matter their lives.

This paper had good service among the people; and Friends have endeavoured much to save the lives of the men in times of wrecks, and to preserve the ships and goods for them. And when some that have suffered shipwreck have been almost dead and starved, some Friends have taken them to their houses to succour and recover them, which is an act to be practised by all true Christians.

Journal pp 179-180 (1660)

We told them that when they went to their sports, and games, and plays, and the like, they had better serve God than spend their time so vainly. And that costly apparel, with the lace that we formerly had

hung upon our backs that kept us not warm, with that
we could maintain a company of poor people that had
no clothes.

Journal p 151 (1657)

... When the time called Christmas came, while
others were feasting and sporting themselves, I would
have gone and looked out poor widows from house to
house, and have given them some money. When I was
invited to marriages (as I sometimes was), I would go
to none at all, but the next day, or soon after, I would go
and visit them: and if they were poor I gave them some
money; for I had wherewith both to keep myself from
being chargeable to others, and to administer
something to the necessities of others.

Journal p 5 1646
(Aged 22)

War and Peace

Friends,
    That which is set up by the sword, is held up by the
sword; and that which is set up by spiritual weapons is
held up by spiritual weapons, and not by carnal
weapons. The peace-maker hath the Kingdom, and is
in it; and hath the dominion over the peace-breaker, to
calm him in the power of God.
    And Friends, let the waves break over your heads.
There is rising a new and living way out of the north,

which makes the nations like waters. The days of virtue, love and peace are come and coming, and the Lamb had and hath the kings of the earth to war, and will overcome by the sword of the Spirit and the word of his mouth.

Letter 4 Ep. 9 (1652)

Commerce and Honesty

And after that riches do increase, take heed of setting your hearts upon them, lest they become a curse and a plague to you. For when ye were faithful at the first, the world would refrain from you, and not have commerce with you; but after, when they saw ye were faithful and just in things, and righteous and honest in your tradings and dealings, then they came to have commerce and trade with you the more, because they know ye will not cheat them. Then ye came to have greater trading, double that ye ever had, and more than the world. But there is the danger and temptation to you, of drawing your minds into your business, and clogging them with it; so that you can hardly do anything to the service of God but there will be crying "My business, my business"; and so therein you do not come into the image of God.

Letter 62 Ep. 131 (1656)

And now that Friends are become a good savour in the hearts of all people, and God having given them his dominion and favour lose it not, but rather increase it in the Life. For at first ye know that many could not take so much money in your trade as to buy bread with. All people stood aloof of you when you stood upright and gave them the plain language and were at a word; but now you, through the Life, come to answer that of God in all, they say they will trust you before their own people, knowing that you will not cheat, nor wrong, nor oppress them. For the cry is now among those that are without; "Where is there a Quaker of such and such a trade?" So that they will deal with Friends before they will deal with their own.

Oh, therefore Friends, who have purchased this through great suffering, lose not this great favour which God hat given unto you, but that you may answer the witness of God in every man, which witnesseth to your faithfulness, that they may glorify your Father on your behalf.

Letter 92 Ep. 251 (1667)

Epistles To Friends

And in your Meetings wait upon the Lord, and take heed of forming words, but mind the Power. So the Lord God of Power be with you all, my dear hearts! I am with you in the spirit, and in the love of your God, your Father and mine. The Love of God is love past knowledge, which bears all things, endures all things, hopes all things, envieth not, thinketh no evil. And the love of God is the ground of all true love in your hearts.

Letter 22 Ep. 43 (1653)

And dear Friends, dwell in the everlasting power of God, that his wisdom you may receive, which is pure and gentle from above, by which all things were made; by which wisdom you may order all things to the glory of God. The poor, the sick, the widows, the fatherless, the prisoners be tender of, and feel every one's condition, as your own, and let nothing be lacking amongst you, according to the apostle's doctrine to the Church of God in old time; and if nothing be lacking, all is well. And the least member in the Church hath an office, and is serviceable; and every member hath need one of another.

Letter 95 Ep. 264 (1669)

To Friends in Barbados

And now Friends, all be careful of God's glory, and seek the good one of another; and strive to be of one mind and heart, and that the peace and gentle wisdom of God may order you all. And be courteous, kind and tender-hearted to one another.

Letter 107 Ep. 315 (1675)

And Friends everywhere, meet together, that your minds may be guided by the spirit of God up to God. And know the life of God in one another.

Letter 25 Ep. 48 (1653)

Mind that which is pure in you, that ye may grow up in the power, out of the form.

Letter 35 Ep. 69 (1654)

... Friends, though ye may have been convinced, and have tasted of the power, and felt the light; yet afterwards ye may feel a winter storm, tempest and hail, frost and cold, and temptation in the wilderness. Be patient and still in the power and in the light that doth convince you, to keep your minds to God; in that be quiet, that ye may come to the summer, that your flight be not in the winter. For if ye sit still in the patience, which overcomes in the power of God, there will be no flying.

Journal p 141 (1657)

Now Friends, who have denied the world's songs and singing, sing ye in the spirit, and with grace, making melody in your hearts to the Lord. And ye having denied the world's formal praying, pray ye always in the spirit, and watch in it. And ye having denied the world's giving of thanks, and their saying of grace and living out of it, do ye in every thing give thanks to the Lord through Jesus Christ. And ye, that have denied the world's praising God with their lips, whilst their hearts are afar off, do ye always praise the Lord night and day. And ye that have denied the world's fastings, and of their hanging down their heads like a bulrush for a day, who smite with the fist of wickedness, keep ye the fast of the Lord, that breaks the bond of iniquity and lets the oppressed go free; that your health may grow, and your Light may shine as the morning.

Letter 74 Ep. 167 (1658)

Friends,

What ye are addicted to, the Tempter will come in that thing; and when he can trouble you, then he gets advantage over you, and then ye are gone. Stand still in that which is pure, after ye see yourselves, and then mercy come in. After thou seest thy thoughts, and the temptation, do not think, but submit, and then power comes. Stand still in that which shows and discovers, and there doth strength immediately come. And stand still in the Light, and submit to it, and the other will be hushed and gone; and then content comes.

Letter 5 Ep. 10 (1652)

Let all nations hear the word by sound or writing. Spare no place, spare not tongue nor pen, but be obedient to the Lord God and go through the world and be valiant for the Truth upon earth; tread and trample all that is contrary under. . . . Be patterns, be examples in all countries, places, islands, nations, wherever you come, that your carriage and life may preach among all sorts of people, and to them; then you will come to walk cheerfully over the world, answering that of God in every one.

(Quoted in Christian Faith and Practice,
Chapter 8, 376) (1656)

On Meetings – Advice and Care to Young and Inexperienced

About this time many mouths were opened in our Meetings to declare the goodness of the Lord, and some that were young and tender in the truth would sometimes utter a few words in thanksgiving and praises to God. That no disorder might arise from this in our meetings, I was moved to write an epistle to Friends by way of advice in that matter . . .:

"All my dear friends in the noble Seed of God, who have known His power, life, and presence among you, let it be your joy to hear or see the springs of life break forth in any: through which ye may have all unity in the same, feeling life and power. And above all things, take heed of judging any openly in your meetings, except they be openly profane or rebellious, such as be out of the truth .... But such as are tender, if they should be moved to bubble forth a few words, and speak in the Seed and Lamb's power, suffer and bear that .... And if they should go beyond their measure, bear it in the meeting for peace and order's sake, and that the spirits of the world be not moved against you. But when the meeting is done, then if any be moved to speak to them, between you and them, one or two of you that feel it in the life, do it in the love and wisdom that is pure and gentle from above: for love is that which doth edify, bears all things, suffers long, and doth fulfil the law."

Journal p 141 1657

Ye that be turned to the Light, walk in the Light, walk in the Truth, where no darkness is; with which Light, that never changeth, ye may come to see that, which was in the Beginning, before the World was, where there is no shadow, nor darkness. In which Light as ye wait, ye will come to receive into your Hearts the word of Faith, which reconciles to God .... Therefore wait in the Light, that ye may receive it, the same Word that ever was, which the Scriptures were given forth from.

So Friends, keep your Meetings, and, as ye are moved of the Lord be obedient to him, and keep your habitations. And be not troubled, but look at that which giveth you to see over the World. So the Lord God Almighty preserve you all to his Glory. Amen.

Day Book of Counsel and Comfort p 71.
(1655)

Letter to Friends in Charleston, South Carolina

For we are here under great persecution. Betwixt thirteen and fourteen hundred in prison, an account of which hath lately been delivered to the King, besides great spoil and havoc which is made of Friends' goods, and beside many are imprisoned and praemunired for not swearing allegiance. And we are kept out of our Meetings in streets and highways in many places of the land, and beaten and abused. Therefore prize the liberty which you enjoy. But the Lord's power is over all, and supports his people.

Letter 126, Ep. 386 (1683)

Letter to Friends in Dantzick

In the love of God and the Lord Jesus Christ, look above all your outward sufferings, and him that is out of Truth that makes you to suffer, and let nothing separate you from the love of God which you have in Christ Jesus. I say, let not carnal weapons, gaols and prisons, threats or reproaches move you, but feel the well of life springing up in you, to nourish the plant that God has planted in you. And therefore let your faith stand in the Lord's power, which is your hedge and defence. And so to the praise and glory of God you may bring forth fresh and green fruit, being grafted onto the Green Tree, that never withers.

Letter 110 Ep. 336 (1676)

And if any servants be convinced, and turned from their places for Truth's sake, Friends be tender to them, that they be not lost, but that they may be preserved. And if any soldiers be put out of the army for Truth's sake, that they may be nourished and cherished; or any children be turned from their parents, or believing wives from their unbelieving husbands, that they may be admonished to walk wisely towards them. And that all prisoners, that have but little of their own, there may be care taken for them, and for the lame and the sick. And that, if any Friends be oppressed any manner of way, others may take care to help them; that all may be as one family, building up one another, and helping one another. . . .

. . . And every one be obedient to the life and power of God, and that will keep you from being as a wilderness, but be faithful and still, till the winds cease, and the storm be over.

Letter 60 Ep. 121 (1656)

To Friends that are Prisoners at York

And though you be in outward bonds from your wives, families, houses and relations, yet the word of God is not bound: It's at liberty; it abides and endures for ever. It will make you all rich, though they think to make you poor with their bonds, and cast you into prisons, but I tell you, the word of God will make you rich, for the word of God was before the wicked and his bonds were; for in the beginning was the word, but since the beginning was the Devil.

In Christ you have heavenly peace; that none can take away from you. In him live and dwell.

Letter 122 Ep. 377 (1682)

All Friends and brethren everywhere, that are imprisoned for the Truth, give yourselves up to it, and it will make you free, and the power of the Lord will carry you over all the persecutors . . . .

Be faithful for the life and power of the Lord God, and for the Truth be valiant upon the earth, and look not at your sufferings, but at the power of God, and that will bring some good out in all sufferings; and your imprisonments will reach to the prisoned, that the persecutor prisons in himself. So be faithful in your sufferings in the power of the Lord, who now suffer by a false priesthood for his tithes, oaths, temples, which have got up since the apostles' day . . . .

. . . And so, be faithful in that which overcomes, and gives victory.

Letter 46 Ep. 92 (1655)

From Swarthmore to Friends in America

And hold fast the hope which anchors the soul, which is sure and steadfast, that you may float above the world's sea; for your anchor holds sure and steadfast in the bottom, let the winds, storms and raging waves rise never so high. And your star is fixed, by which you may steer to the eternal land of rest, and kingdom of God. So, no more but my love to you all.

Letter 106 Ep. 314 (1675)

From Margret Fell's description of George Fox's first coming to Swarthmore

And then he went on and opened the Scriptures, and said, "The Scriptures were the prophets' words and Christ's and the apostles' words, and what as they spoke they enjoyed and possessed and had it from the Lord." And said, "Then what had any to do with the Scriptures, but as they came to the Spirit that gave them birth. You will say, Christ saith this and the apostles say this; but what canst thou say? Art thou a child of Light and hast walked in the Light, and what thou speakest is it inwardly from God?"

Christian Faith and Practice, Section 20

Sources

Hodgkin, L.V., (compiler), *A Day-Book of Counsel and Comfort,* Macmillian and Co Ltd, London, 1937.

London Yearly Meeting of the Religious Society of Friends, *Christian Faith and Practice in the Experience of the Society of Friends,* Headley Brothers Ltd, London, 1960.

Penny, Norman, (editor), *The Journal of George Fox,* J.M. Dent and Sons, London, 1924.

Sharman, Cecil M., (editor), *No More But My Love,* "Letters of George Fox", Quaker Home Service, London 1980.